Let's write!

Liebe Schülerin, lieber Schüler,

mit diesem Heft lernst du, wie man Blogeinträge, E-Mails, Veranstaltungsseiten, Tagebucheinträge, Sorgenbriefe, einfache Bedienungsanleitungen, kurze Vorstellungen von Geschäftsideen und Geschichten schreibt.
Passend zu den *Themes* im Buch gibt es immer ein Textbeispiel. Nach dem Beispiel folgt eine *checklist*, die dir sagt, was du für deinen Text beachten sollst.
Der *language support* hilft dir mit dem Formulieren von Sätzen. Er wird nach und nach erweitert, sodass du hier immer Formulierungen findest, die du schon kennst und andere, die du neu dazulernen kannst.
Die *text frames* unterstützen dich zusätzlich beim Schreiben. Du kannst sie mit deinen Ideen vervollständigen und darfst auch Satzteile wegstreichen, wenn du sie nicht verwenden kannst. Du kannst selbstverständlich auch immer eigene Sätze ergänzen. Wichtig: Übertrage deinen Text zum Schluss in dein Heft.

Hinten im Heft findest du *wordbanks*, die dir helfen, die sprachlichen Anforderungen der Texte zu erfüllen. Außerdem findest du dort sprachliche Hilfen für die Partnerkorrektur oder Schreibkonferenz. Du kannst jeden Text immer mithilfe der *checklist* überprüfen und so hilfreiche Rückmeldung für Mitschülerinnen und Mitschüler geben.
Der *language support* hinten im Heft hilft dir, am Ende der Stunde mit einer Partnerin oder einem Partner darüber zu sprechen, was du gelernt hast und wie sehr du dich bemüht hast.

Die jeweiligen *language support*-Karten können auch als Hilfskarten für die Klassenarbeit verwendet werden. Das entscheidet deine Lehrerin oder dein Lehrer.

Und jetzt: Ganz viel Spaß beim Schreiben!

LET'S WRITE!

1. Plan your writing.
Brainstorm.
Word webs, lists and graphic organisers can help you.

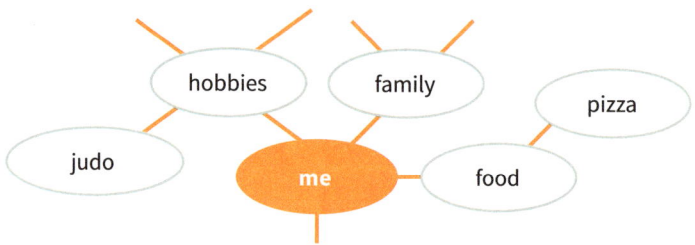

2. Write your first draft.
Read the examples first. You can use checklists, language supports, wordbanks and text frames. You can delete parts in the text frames which don't fit.

My name is Tom.
I'm from Cologne. Cologne is in Germany.
I'm ten years old.
My family is very big. I've got a mum, a dad, a brother and two sisters.
My favourite colour is green.
My hobby is judo.
I've got a cat and a hamster.
My best friends are Anis and Milo.

3. Check your text.
Make your text better!
Checklists can help you to check your text.
Dictionaries can help you to check your spelling.
When you have finished your text in the text frame, copy it into your exercise book.

Checklist

Contents:
- Write your name.
- Say where you are from.
- Say how old you are.
- ...

4. Present your text.
Present!
You can show your text to a partner.
You can hang your text up in class.
Don't forget to give feedback to each other.

INHALT

Themen		Seite
Welcome	All about me	4
Theme 1	1 Let's write a blog entry about sports!	5
	2 Let's write a blog entry about food and restaurants!	8
Theme 2	3 Let's design a page for an event booklet!	11
	4 Let's write an email about a festival!	14
Theme 3	5 Let's write a diary entry!	17
	6 Let's write a letter to an agony aunt!	20
Theme 4	7 Let's write a user manual!	23
	8 Let's write about a new invention!	26
Theme 5	9 Let's write an email about holiday plans!	29
	10 Let's write a story!	32
	Wordbank	36
	Feedback & Talking about goals	38

WELCOME BACK TO CAMDEN MARKET

All about me

All about me!

My name is _____ .   I live in _____ .

I'm _____ years old.   I'm in class _____ .

Favourite sports:

Favourite food:

Favourite restaurant:

What I like about my neighbourhood:

Favourite street festival:

Things for a desert island: **I can't live without this electronic device:**   Top three inventions:

1. _____   1. _____

2. _____   _____   2. _____

3. _____   _____   3. _____

Plans for the holidays: activities and places   Favourite town / country:

ARE YOU FIT? Keeping fit

1 Let's write a blog entry about sports!

Hi everyone!
Today I want to tell you about my favourite sport: Longboard Dancing! It's amazing. You can do so many great things on a longboard!

I started longboarding two years ago. It's like skateboarding but the deck is much bigger so it's easier to ride and keep your balance. I really liked it and after some time I started dancing on the longboard.

To dance on your longboard, you start by walking up and down the board. It's not as easy as you think. It needs a lot of practise but it's so much fun. I have a trainer once a week. His name is Carl and he is a longboard dancing pro. He is the best at showing and explaining dance moves. Thanks to Carl I can even do the Peter Pan move. Here you walk criss cross along your board while riding.

I also practise on my own whenever I find the time. Longboard dancing is great because you can do it whenever you want. You just need a nice pavement. Also make sure there are no cars around. There is a cool place down at the river where some longboard dancers meet. It's always fun to go there. You can check out cool dance moves and everyone is really helpful.

You can come join us any time: all you need is a longboard, a helmet and some protection. If you've never seen longboard dancing, you should definitely check out some videos online.

What is your sport? I can't wait for your comments!

Checklist

Contents:
- Say hello or use a headline.
- Say what you are going to write about.
- Write about your favourite sport.
- Say what you like about your sport.
- Say when you started with your sport.
- Say how often you do your sport.
- List the things you need for your sport.
- Ask questions.
- Finish with a closing phrase.

Language:
- Start your blog (after saying hello) with a capital letter.
- Use time words.
- Use linking words.
- Use adjectives to make your blog more interesting.
- Use paragraphs to make your blog easier to read.

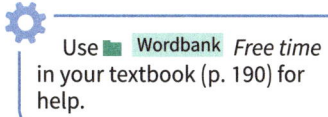

Use Wordbank *Free time* in your textbook (p. 190) for help.

ARE YOU FIT? Keeping fit

Language support

Saying hello:
Hi everyone ! / Hi guys! / Hey there!

Saying what you are going to write about:
Today I'm going to write about … /
I want to share something about … /
Let me tell you about …

Main part:
My favourite sport is … / I enjoy playing/watching … / I really like … /
I like/love it because … it's fast/I meet my friends/
I play in a team/it's really cool/it's great fun/it keeps me fit/it's exciting/
it makes me feel free and happy/you can do it whenever you want/
it keeps you healthy/ …
I think my sport is … /
… is better than … because …
The best part is you can …
I started … months/years ago./ My love for … began … years ago.
I train once/twice/three times/… a week. / I train whenever I can. /
I watch … at the weekends /…
I play/go/do … in a park/sports hall/at the sports ground/on the street/…
I usually wear …
You need … / You just need …

Asking questions:
What is your sport?
Tell me about your favourite sport.
Are you fit?
How do you keep fit? / …

Finishing with a closing phrase:
Come join us!
Follow me for more!
If you have any questions or comments, leave them in the comment section below.
I can't wait for your comments!

ARE YOU FIT? Keeping fit

Text frame

From: bossessockspitsinessixp.com
Reference: My favourite sport

_____ !

Let me tell you about _____ .

My favourite sport is _____ .

I love it because _____ .

I think my sport is better than _____

because _____ .

The best part is you can _____ .

Doesn't that sound cool?!

My love for _____ began _____ ago.

I train _____ .

I play _____ outside/inside.

I usually wear _____ .

You also need _____ .

Come join us! _____ is just _____ !

_____ ?

_____ ?

I can't wait for your comments!

1   ARE YOU FIT? Eating habits

2 Let's write a blog entry about food and restaurants!

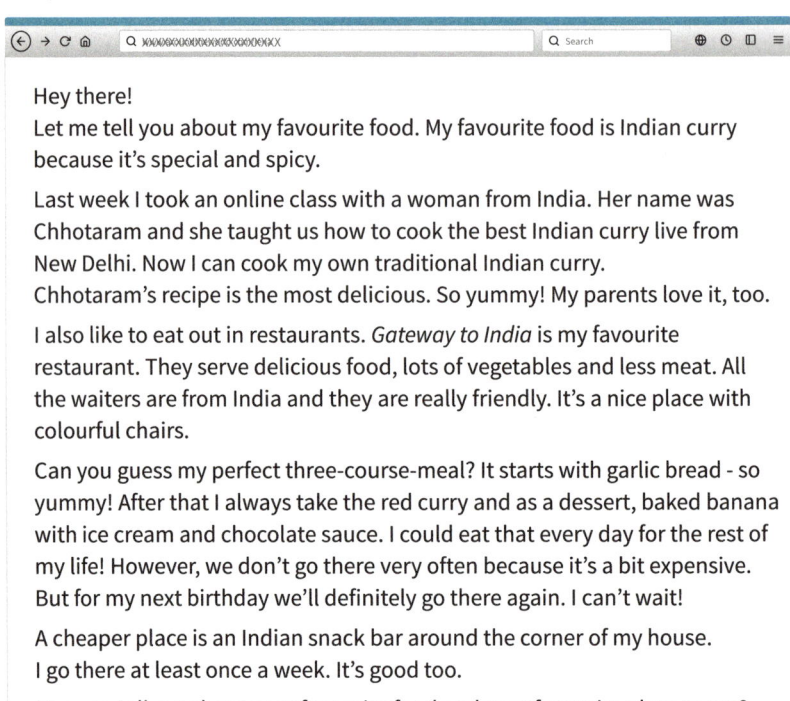

Hey there!
Let me tell you about my favourite food. My favourite food is Indian curry because it's special and spicy.

Last week I took an online class with a woman from India. Her name was Chhotaram and she taught us how to cook the best Indian curry live from New Delhi. Now I can cook my own traditional Indian curry.
Chhotaram's recipe is the most delicious. So yummy! My parents love it, too.

I also like to eat out in restaurants. *Gateway to India* is my favourite restaurant. They serve delicious food, lots of vegetables and less meat. All the waiters are from India and they are really friendly. It's a nice place with colourful chairs.

Can you guess my perfect three-course-meal? It starts with garlic bread - so yummy! After that I always take the red curry and as a dessert, baked banana with ice cream and chocolate sauce. I could eat that every day for the rest of my life! However, we don't go there very often because it's a bit expensive. But for my next birthday we'll definitely go there again. I can't wait!

A cheaper place is an Indian snack bar around the corner of my house.
I go there at least once a week. It's good too.

Can you tell me about your favourite food and your favourite place to eat?
I have to stop now. Today is curry cooking day!

Checklist
Contents:

- Say hello or use a headline.
- Say what you are going to write about.
- Write about your favourite food.
- Say why it is your favourite food.
- Say if you can cook it.
- Write about your favourite restaurant.
- Say how often you eat there.
- Describe your perfect three-course-meal.
- Ask questions.
- Finish with a closing phrase.

Language:

- Start your blog (after saying hello) with a capital letter.
- Use time words.
- Use linking words.
- Use adjectives to make your blog more interesting.
- Use paragraphs to make your blog easier to read.

Use ■ Wordbank *Food and drink* in your textbook (p. 191) for help.

ARE YOU FIT? Eating habits

Language support

Saying hello:
Hi everyone! / Hi guys! / Hey there!

Saying what you are going to write about:
Today I'm going to write about … /
I want to share something about … /
Let me tell you about … / Today I really want to tell you about … / …

Main part:
Let's get right into it.
My favourite food/meal is … because … / I love … because …
It's delicious/yummy/healthy/spicy/sweet/special/ fresh/traditional/sugary/…
I can/can't cook … / I learned how to cook my favourite meal … ago.
The recipe is easy/the best/delicious/so yummy/difficult/ …
My favourite restaurant / place to eat is …
I like the restaurant because …
It is on … / It is near … / They have …
The food is … and the waiters are …
I go there every day / once a week/month/year.
When I go there, I always eat … / I like to drink … / I also love …
My family's favourite food is … because …
Can you guess my perfect three-course-meal?
It starts with … / As a starter I take … / After that I take … / As a main course I have … / As a dessert I have … / Let me finish this perfect meal with …
It is the best! / There is no other place like this! / …

Asking questions:
Can you tell me about your favourite food and your favourite place to eat?
What's your favourite restaurant? What's your perfect three-course-meal? …

Finishing with a closing phrase:
I have to stop now, today is curry cooking day!
You should definitely check out my favourite restaurant. For me it's a five star place!
Cheers to delicious food!
If you have any questions or comments, leave them in the comment section below.
I can't wait for your comments!

1

ARE YOU FIT? Eating habits

Text frame

_____!

Today I'm going to write about _____ and

_____ .

Let's get right into it. My favourite food is _____ because

_____ .

It's _____ . I can/can't cook my favourite

meal. The recipe is _____ .

I also like to eat out in restaurants. My favourite place is _____

_____ . It's near _____

and it's a really _____ restaurant.

The food is _____ and the waiters are

_____ . I go there _____ .

When I go there, I always eat _____ and I drink

_____ . Can you guess my perfect three-course-meal?

As a starter I take _____ .

As a main course I have _____ . Let me finish

this perfect meal with _____ as a dessert.

There is no other place like this!

_____?

_____!

WHAT'S ON NEAR YOU? Things we can do

3 Let's design a page for an event booklet!

The gym club proudly presents:

Mud¹ Race

The school's first mud race

What:
The school's mud race is for everyone who likes to run and is not afraid to get dirty. We will have a spectacular 5 km run with 10 obstacles², lots of mud, and tons of fun!
The money raised will be given to our partner school in Rwanda.

When:
4th May 2022

Where:
Friedrich-Ebert-Schule,
race track, Krankenhausstr. 91

Adults: 6€   **Students:** 3€

Join us for the event of the year!
We take your fun seriously!

¹mud – *Matsch*; ²obstacle – *Hindernis*

Checklist

Contents:
- Find a catchy headline.
- Include all the important information of the event:
  - What?
  - Where?
  - When?
  - How much?
- Make it sound interesting.
- Make it eye-catching.
- Finish with an event slogan.

Language:
- **KISS** - **K**eep **i**t **s**hort and **s**imple

2 WHAT'S ON NEAR YOU? Things we can do

Language support

A to Z event slogans
A great experience every time!
Because your fun is important to us!
Creating the best day ever!
Design your day!
Exciting experience!
Fantastic day out!
Great time!
High five!
It's what we do!
Join us for the event of the year!
Keep calm and party!
Let's get the party started!
Make it happen!
No one does it better!
Our job is to make you happy!
Perfect for you!
Queen of all the events of the year!
Remembered always!
Special to the bone!
Turning a day into an event of a lifetime!
Unforgettable!
Very special!
We Create. You Celebrate.
Xenial[1] people guaranteed!
Your vision. Our plan. Event solutions.
Zany![2]

[1]xenial – *gastfreundlich*; [2]zany – *verrückt*

WHAT'S ON NEAR YOU? Things we can do

Text frame

The _____ proudly presents:

_____

What:
_____
_____
_____
_____

When:
_____

Where:
_____

Adults: _____ €   **Students:** _____ €

_____
_____

2
WHAT'S ON NEAR YOU? Street festivals

4 Let's write an email about a festival!

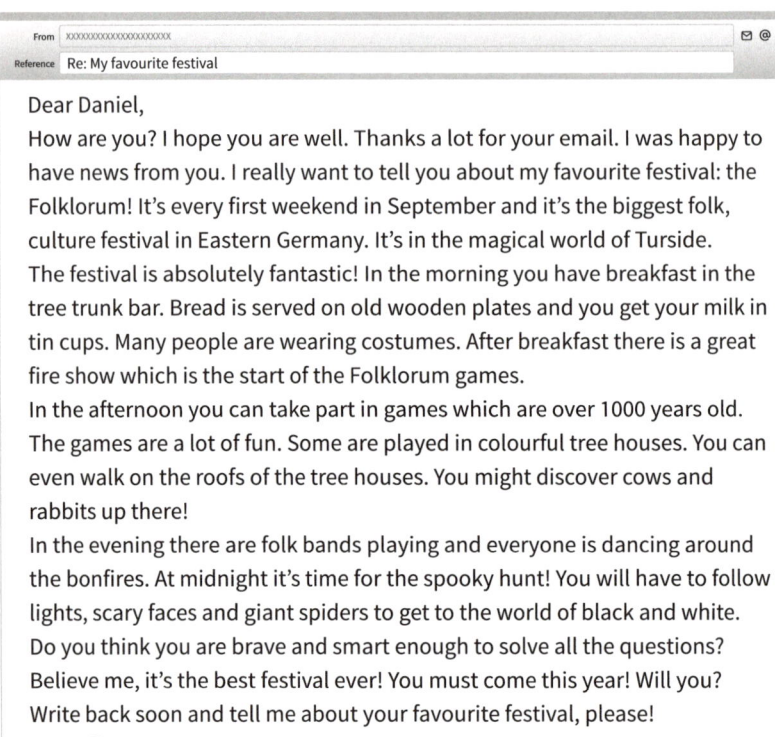

From: XXXXXXXXXXXXXXXXXXX
Reference: Re: My favourite festival

Dear Daniel,
How are you? I hope you are well. Thanks a lot for your email. I was happy to have news from you. I really want to tell you about my favourite festival: the Folklorum! It's every first weekend in September and it's the biggest folk, culture festival in Eastern Germany. It's in the magical world of Turside.
The festival is absolutely fantastic! In the morning you have breakfast in the tree trunk bar. Bread is served on old wooden plates and you get your milk in tin cups. Many people are wearing costumes. After breakfast there is a great fire show which is the start of the Folklorum games.
In the afternoon you can take part in games which are over 1000 years old. The games are a lot of fun. Some are played in colourful tree houses. You can even walk on the roofs of the tree houses. You might discover cows and rabbits up there!
In the evening there are folk bands playing and everyone is dancing around the bonfires. At midnight it's time for the spooky hunt! You will have to follow lights, scary faces and giant spiders to get to the world of black and white.
Do you think you are brave and smart enough to solve all the questions?
Believe me, it's the best festival ever! You must come this year! Will you?
Write back soon and tell me about your favourite festival, please!
Lots of love,
Anne

Checklist

Use 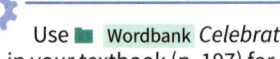 Wordbank *Celebrations* in your textbook (p. 197) for help.

Contents:
- Say hello.
- Start with a friendly first sentence.
- Say what your email is about.
- Give the name of the festival.
- Write about when and where it is.
- Write about the people and the activities at the festival.
- Ask questions.
- Use a closing phrase.
- Say goodbye and write your name.

Language:
- Start your email (after saying hello) with a capital letter.
- Use time words.
- Use linking words.
- Use adjectives and adverbs to make your email interesting.
- Use paragraphs to make your email easier to read.

WHAT'S ON NEAR YOU? Street festivals

Language support

Saying hello:
Hi …, / Hello …, / Dear …,

Starting with a friendly first sentence:
How are you? I hope you're well.
Thank you for your email. / Thanks a lot for your email. / I was happy to have news from you. / I'm very sorry I haven't written for so long … / …

Saying what the email is about:
I'm writing about … / I would like to tell you about … /
You asked me to send you an email about …, so here's some information. /
You asked me some questions about …, so here's what I can tell you.

Main part:
My favourite festival is … / It's a … festival. / It's at the end of … / It's at the beginning of … / It's on (date)(month) … / It takes place in …
In the morning/afternoon/evening …
You can … play games / sing songs / listen to great bands / dance to the music / watch fireworks / talk / shop at the flea market / watch magicians and dancers / get delicious food at different stalls / …
You can eat … and drink… It's delicious / yummy / the best / …
There's always … / People are wearing … / For the festival you need …
It's my favourite festival because there is lots to see and do / it's so exciting / it's so much fun / you meet great people / the food is amazing / the music is brilliant / the visitors are always happy / the costumes are fantastic /…
I can't wait to celebrate … again.

Asking questions:
What about you? / What's your favourite festival and why? / Do you like …? / Believe me, it's the best festival ever! You must come this year! Will you? / …

Finishing with a closing phrase:
Well, that's it for today. / Sorry, I must stop now because … / Write back soon. / I look forward to hearing from you. / I hope to hear from you soon. / …

Saying goodbye and writing your name:
Yours, … / Love, … / Best wishes, … / Bye for now, …

2
WHAT'S ON NEAR YOU? Street festivals

Text frame

_____ ,

_____ ? _____ .

Thank you for _____ . You asked me about _____ . It's _____ !

It's every _____ and it's a _____ festival.

It takes place in _____ . It's _____ !

In the morning there is _____ .

In the afternoon you can _____ .

People _____ and _____ .

You can eat _____ and drink _____ .

In the evening there is _____ .

We often _____ . It's so _____ !

It's my favourite festival because _____ .

We _____ and _____ .

I can't wait to celebrate _____ again!

_____ ? _____ ?

_____ .

_____ ,

_____

YOU'RE NOT ALONE Robinson Crusoe

5 Let's write a diary entry!

> 11th October
>
> Dear diary,
> I'm writing to you from Tropical Island. No, it's not a desert island. It's Europe's largest tropical holiday resort. You can fit the Statue of Liberty or the Eiffel Tower in here! It's AMAZING!
> Today I went swimming and diving. I swam in the blue lagoon, the water falls and the underwater world. It was fantastic! Germany's highest waterslide tower is here, too. Its blue slide speeds up to 70km/h. But I was too scared to try it. Of course, my older sister went. She said it's the best slide ever! I hope I can get myself down there tomorrow.
> My favourite area is the outdoor area. There are many more swimming pools, you can have a picnic on the grass, play beach volleyball or go on the fast whitewater river.
> Mum and Dad spent the day in the sauna & spa area with seven saunas and two steam baths. To me it looked quite boring, but they say it's the perfect place to relax.
> Tonight we will all sleep in a tent at the beach. It's so exciting.
> I will go for a night swim now.
> This is the best day ever!
> Bye for now. I will tell you tomorrow if I tried the waterslide tower.

Checklist
Contents:
- Write the date on the right side.
- Start with *Dear diary,* …
- Think of a special event.
- Keep a logical order.
- Describe details.
- Write about your thoughts and feelings.
- Use exclamations and questions.
- Use comments.
- Say how you feel.
- Finish your diary entry with an interesting sentence or question.
- Use a closing phrase.

Language:
- Write in the first person singular.
- Use time words.
- Use linking words.
- Use adjectives to express your feelings and describe details.

 Use **Wordbank** *People* in your textbook (p. 193) for help.

YOU'RE NOT ALONE Robinson Crusoe

Language support

Saying hello:
Dear diary, …

Starting the diary entry:
Today is … of my life. / I'm writing to you because … /
Something … happened today. / I have to tell you what happened to me today!
Why is this happening to me? / …

Main part:
Writing about feelings:
I feel … / I feel like … / I'm feeling … / I have never felt as … as today. /
Sometimes I still feel …
sad / angry / frustrated / embarrassed / annoyed / scared / afraid / lonely /
nervous / horrible / terrible / unhappy / bad / happy / joyful / great / excited / …

Writing about thoughts:
I really need to … / Maybe … / I think … / I believe … / I must … / I mustn't … /
I can … / I can't … / I should … / I guess … / I'm sure … / I bet … / I wonder … /
I'll have … one day. / I won't … / I can tell you …

Using exclamations and questions:
That's …! / Isn't that just amazing / exciting / fantastic / horrible / terrible / …?
What can I do now? / Can you believe it?

Using comments:
It's horrible! / It's terrible! / HELP! / I hate it!
It's a dream come true! / I'm on cloud nine. / Magical! / I love it!

Finishing:
Let's hope for a miracle. / Is that too much to ask for? /
What a perfect day! This is the best day ever! / Greatest moment of my life!
I'm so very tired … / …

Using a closing phrase:
Bye for now, … / I'll be back tomorrow, … /
Talk to you tomorrow, …

YOU'RE NOT ALONE Robinson Crusoe

Text frame

_____

Dear diary,

I'm so _____ .

Today _____ .

This is what happened: _____ .

_____

_____

_____

That was _____ ! I feel _____ .

I really _____ !

I feel like _____ .

Then there is _____ .

That's _____ .

I wonder what _____ .

I think _____ and

I should _____ .

This is the _____ ever!

_____ !

3 YOU'RE NOT ALONE Dealing with problems

6 Let's write a letter to an agony aunt!

28th October

Dear Holly,

I'm writing to you because I've got a problem with exams. At home I study and I always understand the subject. I can solve every exercise in my textbook or workbook as long as I'm at home. But in an exam I'm totally lost.

Usually I start alright. I read the exercises. I know what to do. I start working, but after half an hour or so I can't concentrate anymore. Then I get nervous and forget everything. It's like my brain just blanks. Then I just sit there, not able to do anything.

I'm quite a good student and I work hard but I never get good marks in my exams. Then my parents get angry with me. They say I'm lazy and I need to study harder. But I'm not lazy and I study a lot. I will lose all my free time if I must study more. And I'm sure studying more won't help. That's not what my problem is about.

What can I do? Please help me. I will be grateful for your advice.

Ben, 13

Checklist

 Use Wordbank *People* in your textbook (p. 193) for help.

Contents:
- Write the date on the right side.
- Say hello.
- Say why you are writing and what your problem is.
- Explain your problem in detail and give examples.
- Use a question to ask for help.
- Say that you are waiting for an answer and that you will be grateful.
- Write your name and age.

Language:
- Start your letter (after saying hello) with a capital letter.
- Use linking words.
- Use adjectives to express your feelings and describe details.
- Use paragraphs to make your letter easier to read.

YOU'RE NOT ALONE Dealing with problems

Language support

Saying hello:
Hi …, / Hello …, / Dear …,

Saying why you are writing and what the problem is:
I'm writing to you today because I hope you can help me with my problem. /
I'm writing to you because … /
I really need your help. /
I need your help because … / …

Main part:
The problem is … / I have a problem with … / My problem is (that) …
It's like this: …
I (don't) want …
So …
I am … / I feel …
I'm really frustrated. / I'm so sad and desperate. / I'm totally lost.
I want this to stop. / I don't like that at all.
I would like to … but …
I'm worried that …
For example …
And I'm sure … won't help. That's not what my problem is about.
I don't know what to do.
Now you know how I feel.

Asking for help:
What can I do? / Can you help me? / Please help me.

Using a closing phrase:
I'm waiting for your answer.
Hope to hear from you asap[1].
I will be really grateful/thankful for your advice.

Writing your name and age:
(name, age)

[1]asap = as soon as possible

3

YOU'RE NOT ALONE Dealing with problems

Text frame

_____

Dear _____ ,

I'm writing to you because I've got a problem with _____

_____ . I really need your help.

The problem is _____ .

It's like this: _____ .

I'm totally lost. I feel _____ and

I'm _____ .

So _____ .

I would like to _____ but _____

_____ . I don't know what to do.

And I'm sure _____ won't help.

That's not what my problem is about.

What can I do? Please _____ . I will be thankful for

your advice.

_____ .

_____

EVERYDAY SCIENCE Digital world

7 Let's write a user manual!

How to make a video call on your mobile phone

This user manual explains how to use the video call app "Face to Face". You can use "Face to Face" to call family and friends or anyone who is in your contact list as long as they have the same app.
The app works on your mobile phone and uses your mobile phone's camera and microphone. You need your mobile phone and the Internet.

Step-by-step instructions:
1. **Download** the app.
2. **Open** the Face to Face app.
3. Tap the **speech bubble icon** in the top right corner.
4. **Choose a contact** from your list.
5. Press the **video camera icon** in the bottom left corner. Your call rings.
6. In a video call you can swap your camera from front to rear by tapping the **rotate icon**. You can show yourself or your surroundings.

Warnings:
- Keep app closed when not in use to not call someone by accident[1].
- Not for children under 3.
- Do NOT play loud background music.
- Do NOT take screenshots without asking.
- Do NOT use fun filters in a serious call.

[1] by accident – *aus Versehen*

Checklist

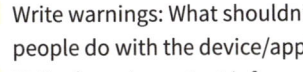
Use Wordbank *Technology* in your textbook (p. 198) for help.

Contents:
- Start with a headline (*How to …*)
- Write a short introduction: What can people do with the device/app?
- Give step-by-step instructions: How can people use the device/app?
- Write warnings: What shouldn't people do with the device/app?
- Write down important information.
- Keep it easy to understand.

Language:
- Use the simple present.
- Use bullet points to make your user manual easier to read.
- Use factual language.
- **KISS** - **K**eep **i**t **s**hort and **s**imple

4 EVERYDAY SCIENCE Digital world

Language support

Starting with a headline:
How to …

Writing a short introduction:
This user manual explains how to …
The app works on/with … / The device works on/with … /
The set consists of: …
You can use … to …
You need …
You also need …
… works with …
Follow these steps to get your … to work.

Giving step-by-step instructions:
Useful verbs:
open / make sure / hold / click / choose / download /
tap[1] / navigate[2] / press / search for / type[3] / log in /
scroll up[4] / scroll down[4] / turn on / turn off /
point / put / turn / pull / push / …

Writing warning:
Keep …
Keep away from …
Not for …
Do NOT …
It's dangerous to …

[1]tap – *klopfen, schlagen*;
[2]navigate – *navigieren, lenken*;
[3]type – *tippen*;
[4]scroll up/down – *vor-/zurückrollen*

EVERYDAY SCIENCE Digital world

Text frame

How to _____

This user manual explains how to _____

_____ . You can use _____

_____ to _____ .

You need: _____

_____

In addition you need: _____ .

Step-by-step instructions:

1. _____

2. _____

3. _____

4. _____

5. _____

Warnings:

- Keep _____ .

- Not for children under _____ .

- Do NOT _____ .

- Do NOT _____ .

- Do NOT _____ .

4

EVERYDAY SCIENCE Inventions

8 Let's write about a new invention!

AMMA – Automatic messaging mum app

How many messages does your mum send you every day? And how much time do you spend answering her? If your answer is a lot to both questions, here is what you need: an app to send automatic messages to your mum. Believe me, this app changed my life.

The app sends pre-programmed messages. You never have to answer a message yourself again. And the best part is that your mum won't know that you haven't sent the message yourself!
All you have to do is create a list that says for example *meeting friends, class, in the park, doing homework*. The program reads your mum's texts and automatically sends the correct answer.
You can even tell the app how fast it should answer to your mum's questions. Of course, this app does not only work for annoying mums but also dads, grandparents, friends …
You can get all this for only 19,99$.

AMMA is a must have for every teenager. Once you try it, you will never want to live without it ever again. Interested? All you have to do is click "buy" now. AMMA will be your new best friend from now on.

Checklist

Contents:
- Start with a catchy headline.
- First, try to get your reader interested in your invention.
- Then sell your product:
  - What can you do with it?
  - What material is it made of?
  - How do you use it?
  - How much is it?
- Ask your reader to buy the invention.

Language:
- Use adjectives to describe your idea.
- Use linking words.
- Use strong and convincing phrases.
- Use paragraphs to make your text easier to read.

 Use **Wordbank** *Technology* and *Things* in your textbook (p. 198ff.) for help.

EVERYDAY SCIENCE Inventions

Language support

Headline
Getting your reader interested:
Hello, have you got a minute?
Let me introduce myself. My name is … / I'm … and this is my fantastic idea: …
Believe me, this … changed my life.
I'm really excited to …
I'm sure you have never heard of …
Have you ever …?
Here is what you need: …
Let me tell you about …

Selling your product:
Here you can see our invention. It is called …
With this invention you can …
It is used to …
My / Our invention is made of…
It works like this: you put … Then you …
What do you think about it?
It's perfect to … / It's the best way to …
It's the ideal solution to …
… makes you feel …
You can …
Of course, it works …
You never have to be / feel … again.
And the best part is …
And if you like it, …
It's only … $. / You can get all this for only … $.

Asking your reader to buy the invention:
… was a life changer for me.
Once you try it, …
If you want to …, all you need to do is to …
It's a must-have.
Wait until you get your hands on …
You will never want to live without it ever again.
Interested? All you have to do is …

4
EVERYDAY SCIENCE Inventions

Text frame

_____ – _____

Hello, have you got a minute?

Let me introduce myself. My name is _____ .

I'm _____ and this is my fabulous idea:

_____ .

Let me tell you some more about it.

My invention is called _____ .

It is made of _____ . With this invention you

can _____ .

It works like this: you put _____ .

Then you _____ .

It's perfect to _____ .

You never have to _____ again.

And the best part is _____ .

It's only _____ $.

If you ask me it's a must have for _____ .

Once you try it, _____ . Interested?

All you have to do is _____ !

UP AND AWAY Planning a holiday

9 Let's write an email about holiday plans!

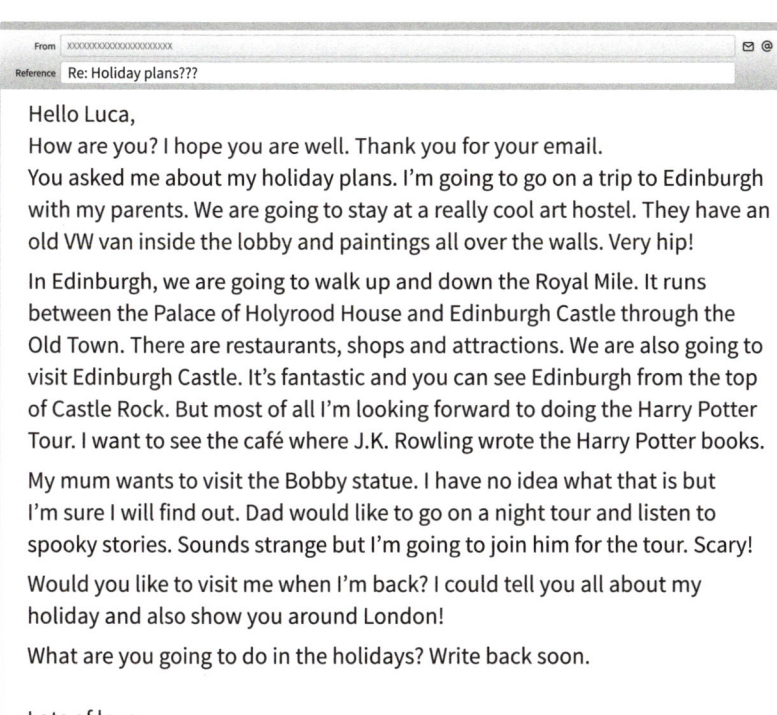

From: XXXXXXXXXXXXXXXXXX
Reference: Re: Holiday plans???

Hello Luca,

How are you? I hope you are well. Thank you for your email.

You asked me about my holiday plans. I'm going to go on a trip to Edinburgh with my parents. We are going to stay at a really cool art hostel. They have an old VW van inside the lobby and paintings all over the walls. Very hip!

In Edinburgh, we are going to walk up and down the Royal Mile. It runs between the Palace of Holyrood House and Edinburgh Castle through the Old Town. There are restaurants, shops and attractions. We are also going to visit Edinburgh Castle. It's fantastic and you can see Edinburgh from the top of Castle Rock. But most of all I'm looking forward to doing the Harry Potter Tour. I want to see the café where J.K. Rowling wrote the Harry Potter books.

My mum wants to visit the Bobby statue. I have no idea what that is but I'm sure I will find out. Dad would like to go on a night tour and listen to spooky stories. Sounds strange but I'm going to join him for the tour. Scary!

Would you like to visit me when I'm back? I could tell you all about my holiday and also show you around London!

What are you going to do in the holidays? Write back soon.

Lots of love,

Alessio

Checklist

Use **Wordbank** *Travelling* in your textbook (p. 194) for help.

Contents:
- Say hello.
- Start with a friendly first sentence.
- Say what your email is about.
- Write about where you are going to go and stay and who is going with you.
- Say what you are going to do.
- Write about what you are looking forward to doing.
- Use comments.
- Ask questions.
- Use a closing phrase.
- Say goodbye and write your name.

Language:
- Start your email (after saying hello) with a capital letter.
- Use the *going to*-future.
- Use time words and linking words.
- Use adjectives and adverbs to make your email interesting.
- Use paragraphs to make your email easier to read.

5 UP AND AWAY Planning a holiday

Language support

Saying hello:
Hi …, / Hello …, / Dear …,

Starting with a friendly first sentence:
How are you? I hope you're well. / Thank you for your email. /
Thanks a lot for your email. I was happy to have news from you.
I'm very sorry I haven't written for so long. /…

Saying what your email is about:
I'm writing about … / I would like to tell you about … /
I promised to send to you an email about …, so here's some information. /
You asked me (some questions) about … / I really want to tell you about …

Main part:
I'm going to go on a trip to … / I'm going to stay at home.
… is going to go with me. We are going to go there by car/train/bus/plane/…
I am/We are going to stay at / sleep in a hotel/hostel/apartment/caravan/ …
I'm going to visit …
I/We would like to … (but) … / I/We really want to …
My/Our plans are to … / We are also going to …
I really like … / I love … / I enjoy … because …
Most of all I'm looking forward to …
… is the best!

Using comments:
Very hip! / That's pretty cool/special/spectacular …! / Fantastic! /
Amazing! / Sounds great! / That's way too scary! / Isn't that great?!

Asking questions:
What about you? / What are you going to do? / Please tell me about your plans
for the holidays. / What are you most looking forward to?

Using a closing phrase:
Well that's it for today. / Sorry, I must stop now because … /
Write back soon. / I hope to hear from you soon. /
I look forward to hearing from you. /
Hugs and kisses.

Saying goodbye and writing your name and age:
Yours,… / Love, … / Lots of love, … / Best wishes, … / Bye for now, …

UP AND AWAY Planning a holiday

Text frame

_____ ,

_____ ? _____ .

Thank you for _____ . You asked me about _____

_____ so here's what I can tell you.

I _____ .

_____ are going to go with me. We are going

to go there by _____ . We are going to stay _____

_____ . That's _____ !

In the morning we are going to _____ .

In the afternoon _____ .

Isn't that _____ ? We are also going to _____

_____ . I would really like to _____ because

_____ . In the evenings _____

_____ . But most of all I'm looking forward to

_____ . _____ is just the best!

_____ ? _____ ?

_____ .

_____ ,

_____

UP AND AWAY Let's go to Scotland!

10 Let's write a story!

Greyfriars Bobby: story of a dog

This is a true story of a Skye Terrier[1] called Bobby.

In the year 1850 a man called John Gray arrived in Edinburgh, Scotland, with his wife and son. The times were difficult and there were no jobs. John Gray was a gardener, but there was no job for him. So he had to take a job as a police night watchman[2].

Edinburgh's streets at night were very dangerous and lonely. John, however, took his young dog Bobby, the Skye Terrier, with him. The nights were cold, dark and scary, but Bobby protected John and always barked when John was in danger. They were the best team for two years!
Until …

John got ill and died. Bobby couldn't protect him from getting ill. John was buried[3] in Greyfriars graveyard[4] in 1858 and Bobby was very sad. The dog lay down on John's grave[5].

Bobby lay on John's grave for the rest of the day and the next day and the next day and the day after that. Not even in the most terrible weather would the dog get up. The graveyard's keeper carried Bobby away many times because he didn't want him there. But Bobby always came back. Finally, the keeper built a little hut for Bobby. Every day at one o'clock there was a gun sound. Right at that time Bobby left his place. He went to the coffee house where he had gone so often with John. There William Dow, one of his many new friends, gave him food.

Bobby stayed by John's side for 14 years. Can you imagine? He only left him for lunch at one o'clock. The dog died in 1872.

Today you can see a statue of Bobby, the Skye Terrier, right at the graveyard. Bobby's gravestone says: "Greyfriars Bobby – died 14th January 1872 – aged 16 years – Let his loyalty[6] and devotion[7] be a lesson to us all".

[1] Skye Terrier – *bestimmte Hunderasse*;
[2] watchman – *Wachmann*;
[3] buried – *begraben*;
[4] graveyard – *Friedhof*;
[5] grave – *Grab*;
[6] loyalty – *Treue*;
[7] devotion – *Zuwendung*

UP AND AWAY Let's go to Scotland!

Checklist

Contents:
- Give your story a good headline.
- Make sure that your story has got an introduction, a main part and an ending.
- Start with an interesting beginning.
- Answer the wh-questions:
  - What?
  - Who?
  - Where?
  - When?
- Make sure that your story is interesting to read.
- Keep a logical order.
- Describe the situation and feelings.
- Use vivid[1] details.

Language:
- Use the simple past.
- Use time words.
- Use linking words.
- Use adjectives and adverbs to make your story more interesting.
- Use direct speech if needed.
- Use paragraphs to make your story easier to read.

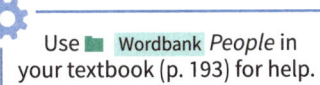

Use Wordbank *People* in your textbook (p. 193) for help.

[1] vivid – *lebendig*

UP AND AWAY Let's go to Scotland!

Language support

	language support	your ideas
Who was in your story?	…, …, … … was with him / her.	
When did the story take place?	It was …	
Where did the story take place?	It all happened in …	
What happened?	He / She saw / decided to / had to … He / She thought: "…" Suddenly … He / She felt … because …	
What happened then?	It was amazing / scary / strange / … He / She … but he / she … When he / she talked to …, he / she … He / She said /screamed: "…" Then …	
And then?	After that … / Later …	
How did it end?	Finally / In the end / … He / She was … One day … It's always good to …	

UP AND AWAY Let's go to Scotland!

Graphic organiser – story map

Title: _____

Who was in your story?
_____
_____
_____

Where did the story take place?
_____
_____
_____

When did the story take place?
_____
_____

What happened?
_____
_____
_____

What was the problem?
_____
_____
_____

How was the problem solved?
_____
_____
_____

WORDBANK

Linking words

and | or | but | so | because | because of this | that's why | …

Time words

in the morning / afternoon / evening | at the weekend | on Monday | (three days) ago | before/after school | first | then | after (that) | afterwards | later | today | yesterday | last Tuesday/year | next week/year | now | at … o'clock | at the moment | every day | finally | …

Adverbs of frequency

never

sometimes

often/usually

always

Comments

I love it! | So sweet! | So beautiful! | Oh my god! | Wonderful! | Magical! | It always makes me smile! | Surprise! | Pretty cool! | Very hip! | …

Horrible! | Terrible! | Oh my god! | Help! | Oh no! | That's too bad! | I hate it! | Sounds strange! | Too scary! | That's horrible/terrible/scary/ …! | …

WORDBANK

Adjectives

funny | great | exciting | beautiful |
wonderful | amazing | hot | warm |
lovely | magical | different | nice |
fantastic | brilliant | quiet | colourful |
clever | interesting | easy | relaxing |
fast | healthy | bright | spectacular | …

bad | boring | cold | loud | terrible |
dangerous | angry | lonely | unhappy |
worried | sad | nervous | afraid | spooky |
scared | tired | ill | upset | horrible |
empty | strange | unhealthy | …

Feelings

I'm feeling great!

positive	negative
excited	happy		desperate	shocked	
good	great		helpless	homesick	
wonderful	glad		bad	bored	lonely	
fantastic	proud	…	nervous	unhappy	
	worried	scared	
	angry	embarrassed	
	afraid	upset	tired	
	frustrated	sad	…

I like … | I love … | I enjoy …
I don't like … | I can't stand … | I hate …

FEEDBACK & TALKING ABOUT GOALS

Symbols to check your first draft

++ (This is good!)
?? (I don't understand this.)
~~ (I don't think this English is correct.)

Feedback

Remember to say something positive!

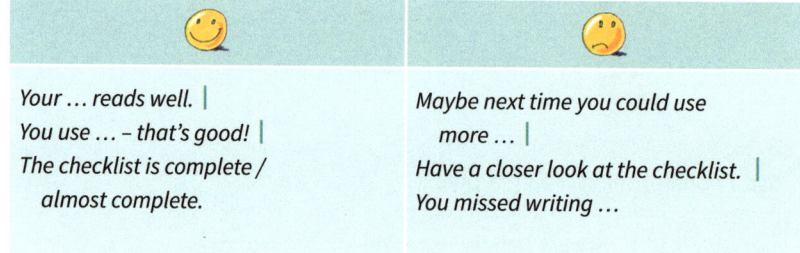

🙂	🙁
Your … reads well. | You use … – that's good! | The checklist is complete / almost complete.	Maybe next time you could use more … | Have a closer look at the checklist. | You missed writing …

Talking about goals

What did you learn today? — Today I learned to write about …

What are you proud of today? — I was good at …

Which support helped you most? — The … was most helpful for me.

What would you like to do better next time? — My goal for next time is to **do a difficult task / concentrate on the task / pay attention / stick to the rules / help my partner / ask for help / listen to Mr / Mrs … / my classmates / try harder / finish my work / start right away / deal with problems / use support / check my writing carefully / use the checklist / …**

Autorin: Daniela Byvank

Bildquelle: |iStockphoto.com, Calgary: monkeybusinessimages Titel.

westermann GRUPPE
© 2022 Westermann Bildungsmedien Verlag GmbH, Georg-Westermann-Allee 66, 38104 Braunschweig
www.westermann.de

Das Werk und seine Teile sind urheberrechtlich geschützt. Jede Nutzung in anderen als den gesetzlich zugelassenen bzw. vertraglich zugestandenen Fällen bedarf der vorherigen schriftlichen Einwilligung des Verlages. Nähere Informationen zur vertraglich gestatteten Anzahl von Kopien finden Sie auf www.schulbuchkopie.de.
Für Verweise (Links) auf Internet-Adressen gilt folgender Haftungshinweis: Trotz sorgfältiger inhaltlicher Kontrolle wird die Haftung für die Inhalte der externen Seiten ausgeschlossen. Für den Inhalt dieser externen Seiten sind ausschließlich deren Betreiber verantwortlich. Sollten Sie daher auf kostenpflichtige, illegale oder anstößige Inhalte treffen, so bedauern wir dies ausdrücklich und bitten Sie, uns umgehend per E-Mail davon in Kenntnis zu setzen, damit beim Nachdruck der Verweis gelöscht wird.

Druck A[1] / Jahr 2022
Alle Drucke der Serie A sind im Unterricht parallel verwendbar.

Redaktion: Demet Kömür
Illustrationen: Ulf Marckwort, Kassel
Umschlaggestaltung: LIO Design GmbH, Braunschweig
Layout: JANSSEN KAHLERT Design & Kommunikation GmbH, Hannover
Druck und Bindung: Westermann Druck GmbH, Georg-Westermann-Allee 66, 38104 Braunschweig

ISBN 978-3-14-**149402**-0